W9-ACQ-882

MAKE IT YOURSELF!

COMICS &
GRAPHIC NOVELS

Christa Schneider

Checkerboard
Library

An Imprint of Abdo Publishing
abdopublishing.com

abdopublishing.com

Published by Abdo Publishing, a division of ABDO, PO Box 398166, Minneapolis, Minnesota 55439. Copyright © 2018 by Abdo Consulting Group, Inc. International copyrights reserved in all countries. No part of this book may be reproduced in any form without written permission from the publisher. Checkerboard Library™ is a trademark and logo of Abdo Publishing.

Printed in the United States of America, North Mankato, Minnesota
062017
092017

THIS BOOK CONTAINS
RECYCLED MATERIALS

Design: Sarah DeYoung, Mighty Media, Inc.
Production: Mighty Media, Inc.
Editor: Liz Salzmann
Cover Photographs: Mighty Media, Inc.
Interior Photographs: iStockphoto; Mighty Media, Inc.; Shutterstock; Thinkstock

The following manufacturers/names appearing in this book are trademarks: Craft Smart®, Crayola®, Elmer's®, Faber-Castell®, Fellowes®, Scotch®, Sharpie®, Strathmore®

Publisher's Cataloging-in-Publication Data
Names: Schneider, Christa, author.
Title: Make it yourself! comics & graphic novels / by Christa Schneider.
Other titles: Make it yourself! comics and graphic novels | Comics and
    graphic novels
Description: Minneapolis, MN : Abdo Publishing, 2018. | Series: Cool
    makerspace | Includes bibliographical references and index.
Identifiers: LCCN 2016962822 | ISBN 9781532110696 (lib. bdg.) |
    ISBN 9781680788549 (ebook)
Subjects: LCSH: Makerspaces--Juvenile literature. | Handicraft--
    Juvenile literature.
Classification: DDC 680--dc23
LC record available at http://lccn.loc.gov/2016962822

TO ADULT HELPERS

This is your chance to assist a new maker! As children learn to use makerspaces, they develop new skills, gain confidence, and make cool things. These activities are designed to help children create projects in makerspaces. Children may need more assistance for some activities than others. Be there to offer guidance when they need it. Encourage them to do as much as they can on their own. Be a cheerleader for their creativity.

Before getting started, remember to lay down ground rules for using tools and supplies and for cleaning up.

CONTENTS

What's a
MAKERSPACE?

Imagine a space buzzing with creativity. All around you people are sketching, coloring, and dreaming up new characters. Wide-open spaces invite you to plan, sketch, and draw. Paper, pencils, markers, crayons, and art supplies are all around you. Any material you could imagine is within reach!

This is a makerspace. It is a place where people come together to create all kinds of cool stuff. Makers share sparks of creativity. They love to learn something new. They work together to design and create amazing comic and **graphic novel** projects. Are you ready to become a maker?

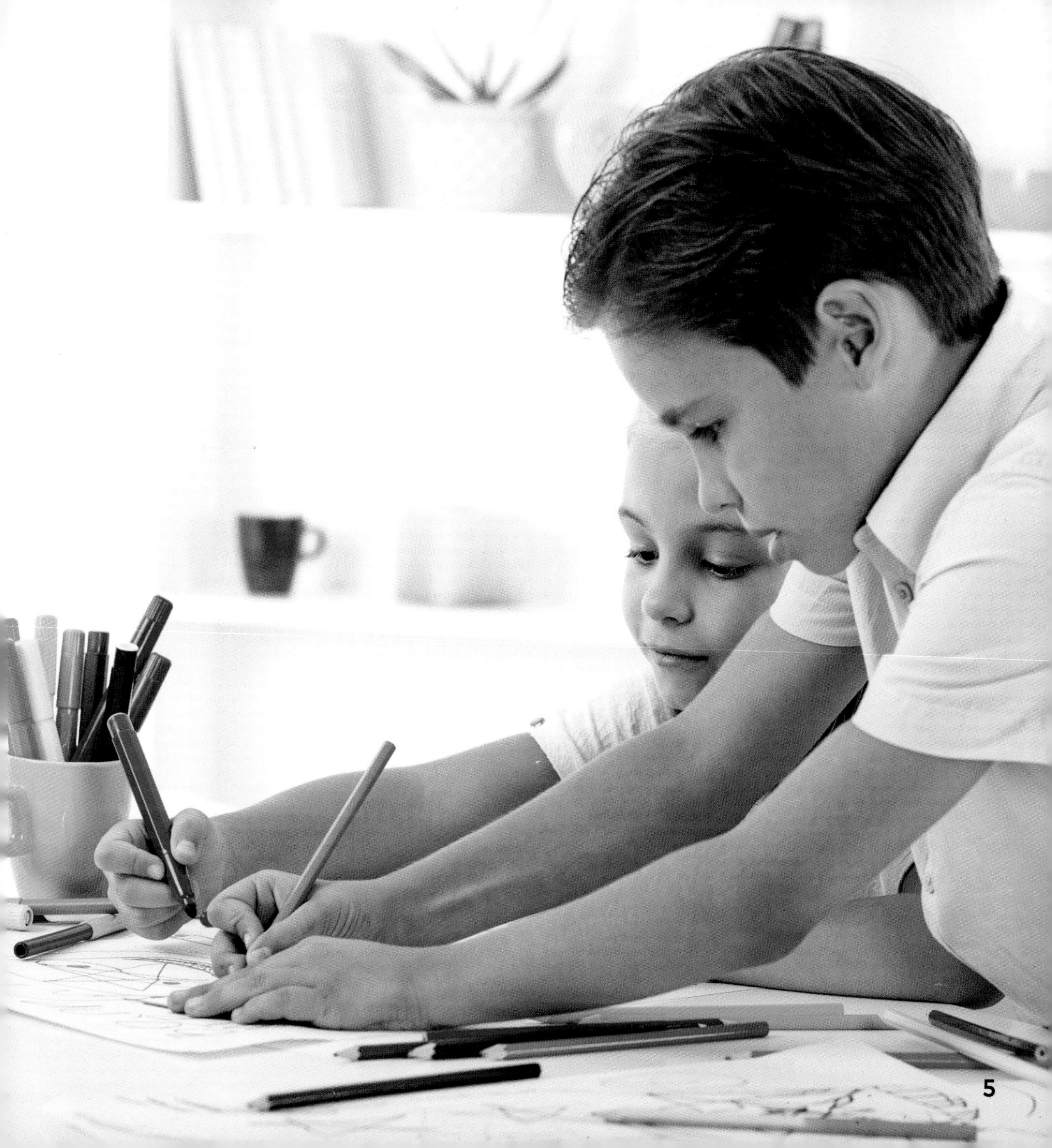

FUN WITH COMICS & GRAPHIC NOVELS

Supplies are an important part of any makerspace. Get inspiration from the materials that surround you! Some projects can be shaped by the supplies you have on hand. Others will call for specific materials.

Don't worry if your makerspace doesn't have a certain material you need. Makers are problem-solvers too! Just find another supply to replace your missing materials. You'll be back to crafting cool comics and great **graphic novels** in no time.

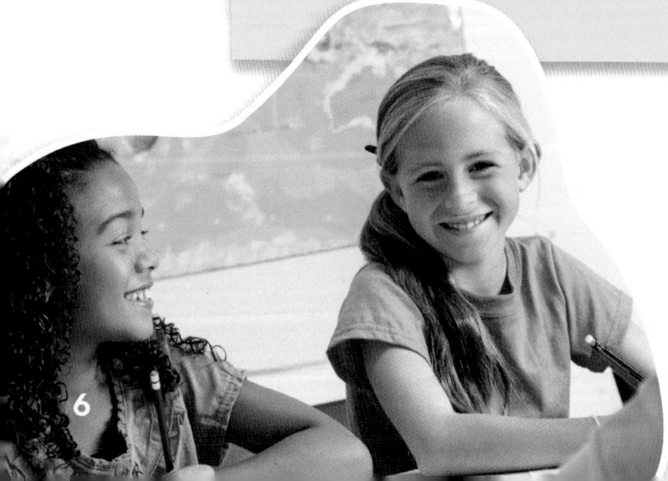

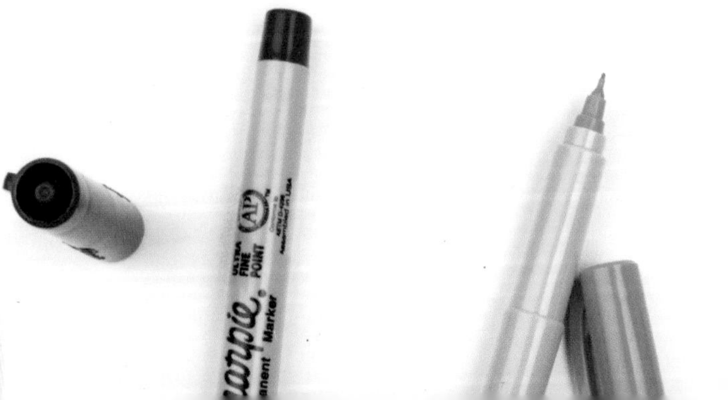

COMIC & GRAPHIC NOVEL TIPS

Sharing is an important aspect of a makerspace. Makers share workspace, materials, and ideas. Being surrounded by other makers is great for creativity. But it also means a lot of projects may be happening at once. Here are some tips for successful makerspace projects.

HAVE A PLAN

Read through a project before beginning. Research any terms you may not know. Make sure you have everything you need for the project.

ASK FOR PERMISSION

Get **permission** from an adult to use the space, tools, and supplies.

BE RESPECTFUL

Before taking a tool or material, make sure another maker isn't using it.

KEEP YOUR SPACE CLEAN

It takes a lot of paper to make a comic or **graphic novel**. Keep your papers organized so they don't get lost. Store pens, pencils, and other art supplies in bins so they don't roll away.

EXPECT MISTAKES & BE CREATIVE

Being a maker isn't about creating something perfect. Have fun as you work!

SUPPLIES

Here are some of the materials and tools you'll need to do the projects in this book.

acrylic paint

blue pencil

Scotch

clear tape

colored pencils

computer

Drawing

drawing paper

erasers

glue stick

inking pens

newspaper

notebook

Sharpie
Sharpie

paint pens

paintbrushes

paper pocket folder

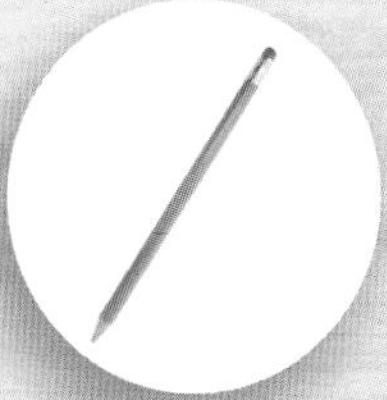

pencil

pens

photocopier

printer

ruler

scissors

self-adhesive laminating sheets

stapler

COMIC & GRAPHIC NOVEL TECHNIQUES

A ruler is helpful for making **panel** borders line up and look sharp. You can also use a ruler to sketch **baselines** for your text to keep it straight.

concert
ARE AROUND THE
corner

Depth can be shown by changing the thickness of your ink lines. The closer an object is to the viewer, the thicker the lines of that object should be.

SPLASH
TSCHI
TSCHI

COMIC CHARACTER COLLECTOR CARDS

Craft a cool card with your very own character!

WHAT YOU NEED

drawing paper

scissors • pencil

inking pen • eraser

colored pencils

self-adhesive laminating sheets

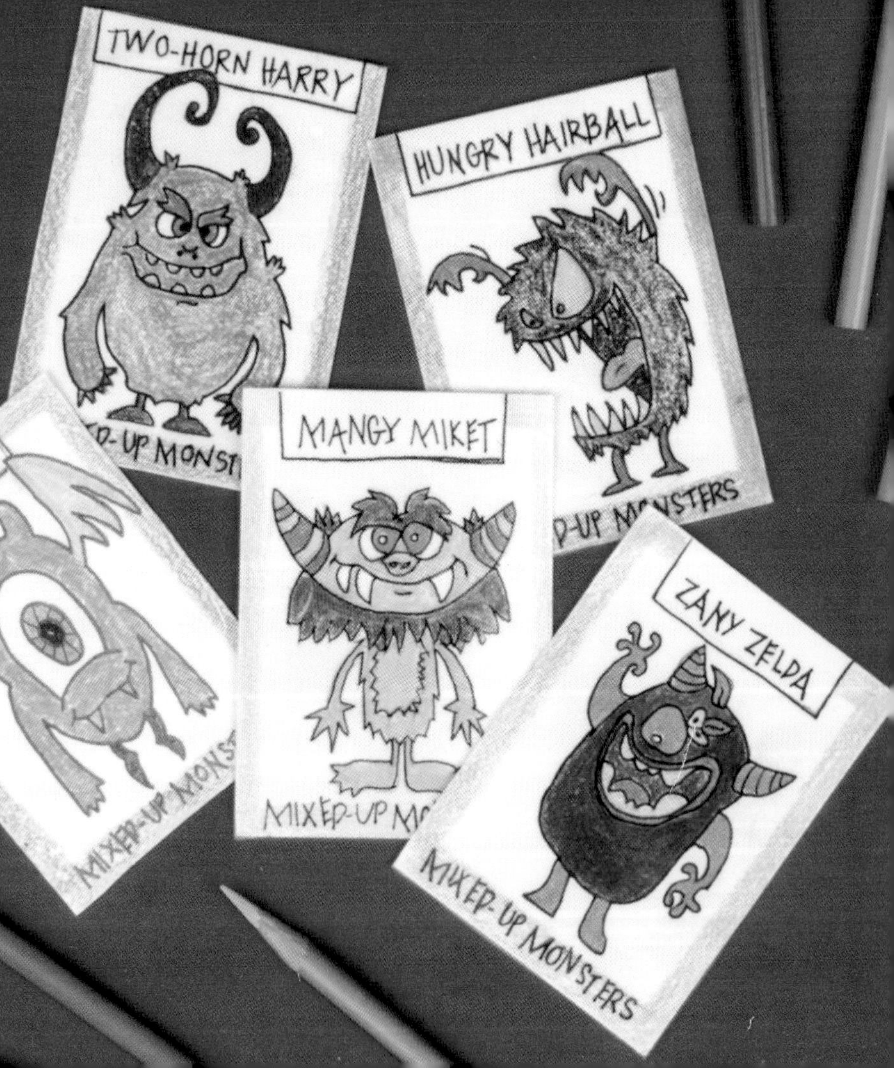

TWO-HORN HARRY
HUNGRY HAIRBALL
MANGY MIKE T
BIG EYE IRIS
ZANY ZELDA
MIXED-UP MONSTERS

1. Fold a sheet of drawing paper into thirds.

2. Fold it into thirds in the other direction.

3. Cut off all four edges of the folded paper. This creates nine cards.

4. Sketch your character and its name on the front of a card. Use light pencil strokes.

Continued on the next page.

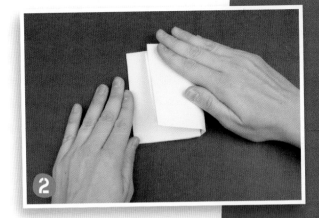

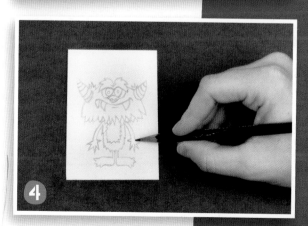

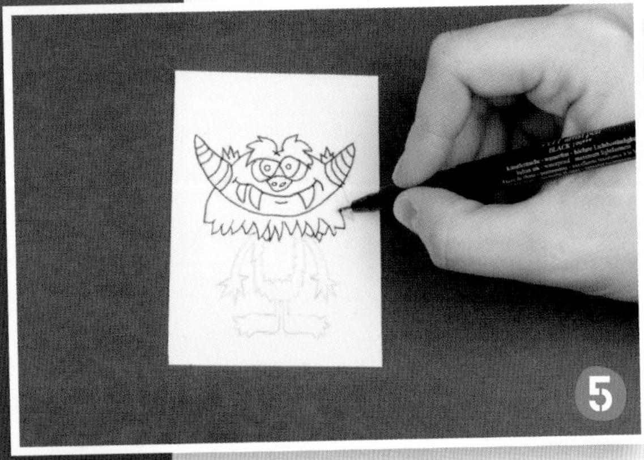
5

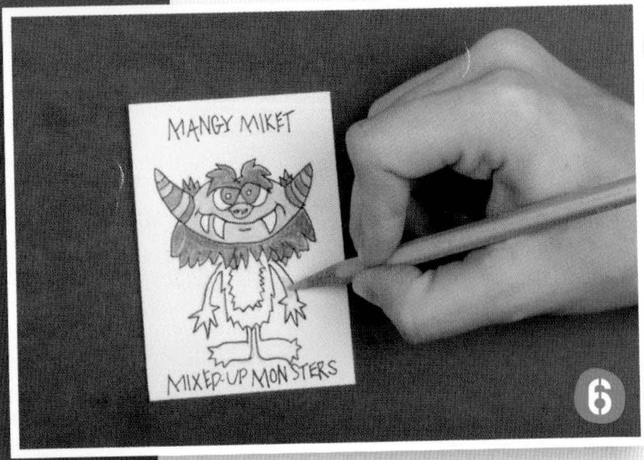
MANGY MIKET
MIXED-UP MONSTERS
6

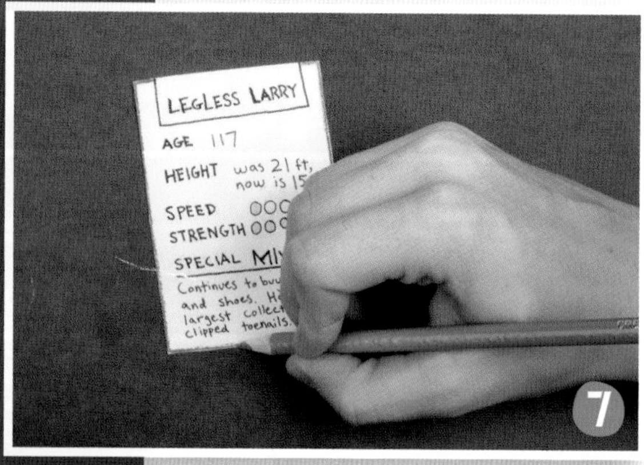
LEGLESS LARRY
AGE 117
HEIGHT was 21 ft,
now is
SPEED
STRENGTH
SPECIAL
Continues to
and shoes.
largest
clipped toenails.
7

5. Trace over the sketch with an inking pen. Let the ink dry. Erase the pencil lines.

6. Use colored pencils to color in the character.

7. Write information about the character on the back of the card. Use colored pencils to add some color, such as a border.

8. Repeat steps 4 through 7 to make eight more cards. Use additional sheets of paper to create as many character cards as you want!

9. Peel back half of the backing of a **laminating** sheet. Place three cards on the exposed half. Do not overlap the cards.

10. Carefully remove the backing entirely. Fold the other half of the laminating sheet over the cards. Smooth it out from the center.

11. Cut the cards out of the laminating sheet.

12. Repeat steps 9 through 11 to laminate the remaining cards.

TIP If you have a corner punch, you can create rounded corners. This will give your cards a more finished look.

HAND-LETTERED PROMO POSTER

Make an eye-catching poster about a concert or other event!

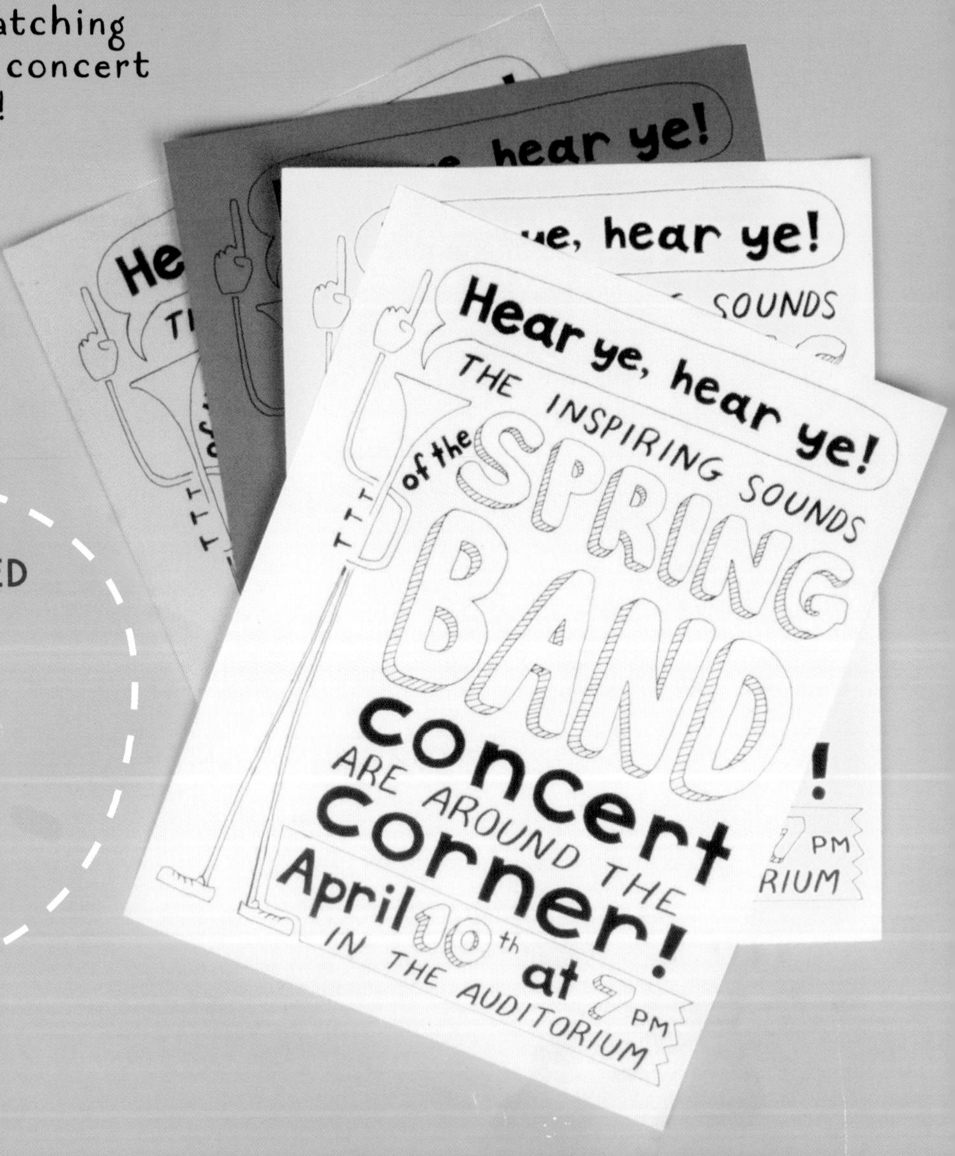
Hear ye, hear ye!
THE INSPIRING SOUNDS
of the
SPRING
BAND
concert
ARE AROUND THE
corner!
April 10th at 7 PM
IN THE AUDITORIUM

WHAT YOU NEED

- pencil
- plain paper
- drawing paper
- blue pencil
- inking pens
- photocopier or scanner & printer

1. Draw several lettering styles for the poster. One should be large to grab people's attention. Use it for the most important words. Draw other styles for the rest of the poster text.

2. Write down all of the information that will be on the poster. Choose which style of text to use for each part.

3. Think of a fun illustration that could have a speech bubble. Decide what text to put in the bubble.

4. Sketch the **layout** of the poster in blue pencil on drawing paper. Start with the illustration and speech bubble. Add the rest of the poster's text. Is there some text that could be inside a frame? Frames help separate information.

5. Trace over the pencil lines with an inking pen.

6. Make copies of your poster. Ask if you can post them at school and around your neighborhood!

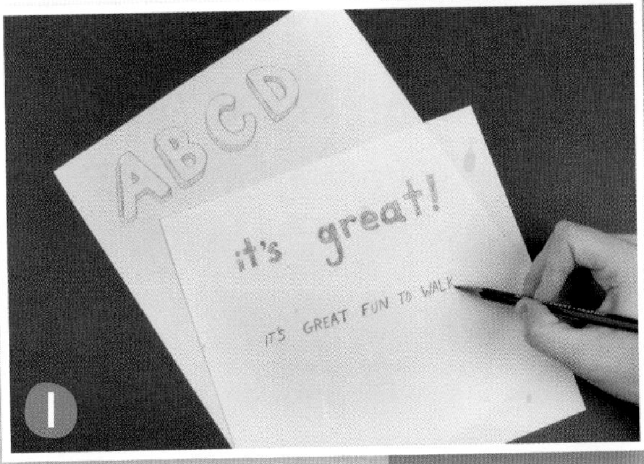
ABCD
it's great!
IT'S GREAT FUN TO WALK
1

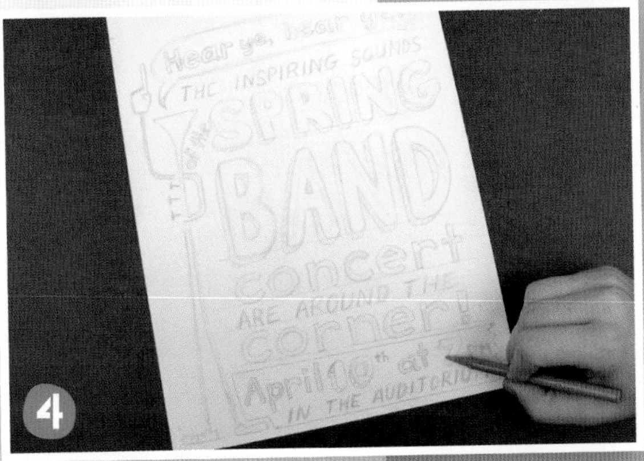
THE INSPIRING SOUNDS
SPRING
BAND
concert
ARE AROUND THE
corner!
4

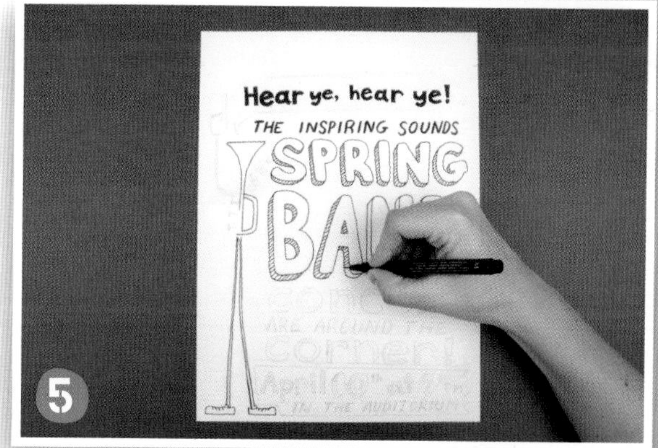
Hear ye, hear ye!
THE INSPIRING SOUNDS
SPRING
ARE AROUND THE
corner!
5

CUT-AN-INVITE

Make a cool comic strip invitation!

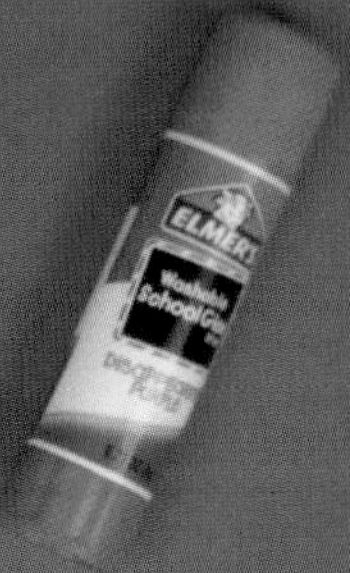

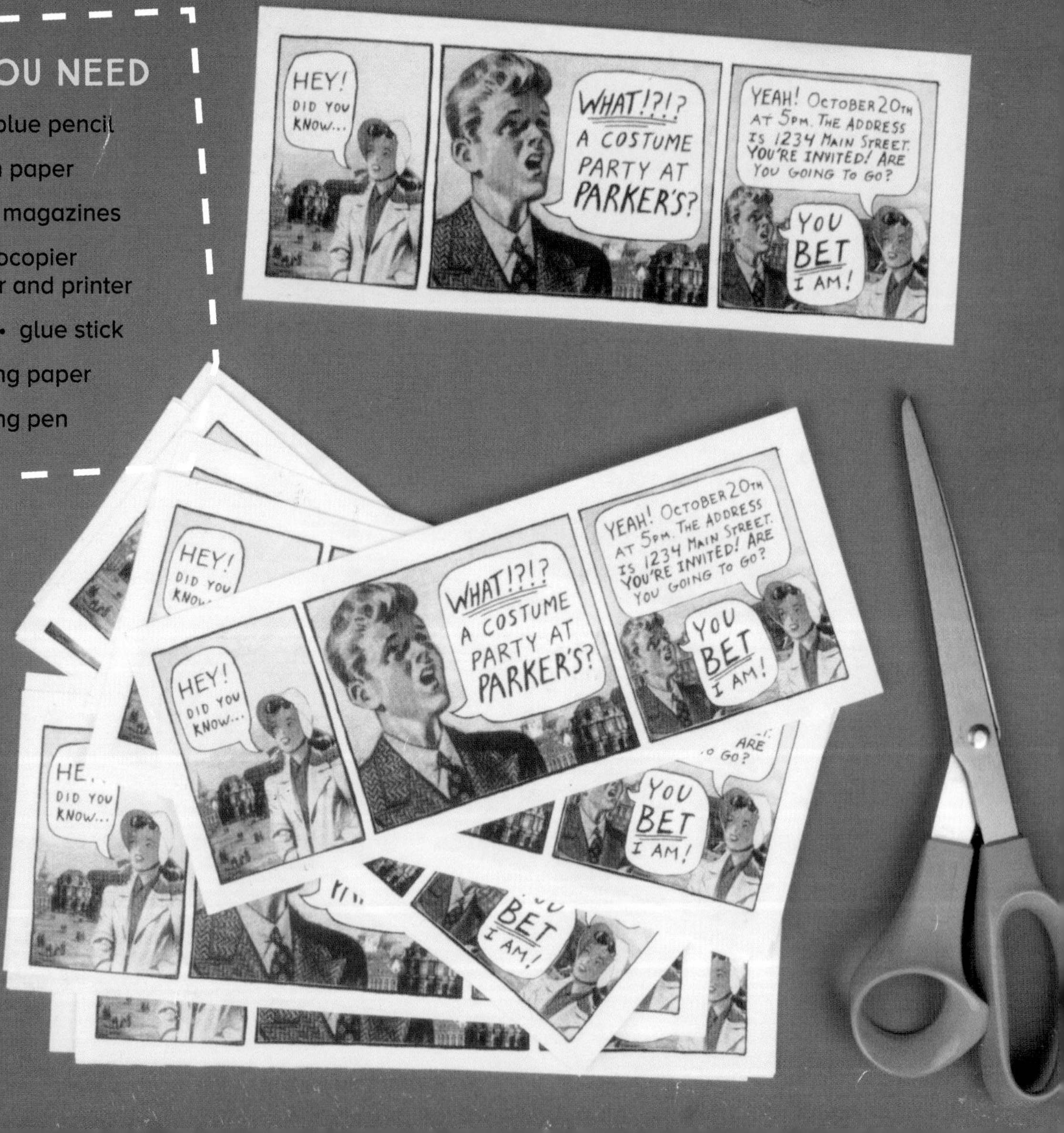
HEY! DID YOU KNOW...
WHAT!?!? A COSTUME PARTY AT PARKER'S?
YEAH! OCTOBER 20TH AT 5PM. THE ADDRESS IS 1234 MAIN STREET. YOU'RE INVITED! ARE YOU GOING TO GO?
YOU BET I AM!

WHAT YOU NEED

ruler • blue pencil

plain paper

books or magazines

photocopier
or scanner and printer

scissors • glue stick

drawing paper

inking pen

1. Use a ruler and blue pencil to draw three **panels** on a sheet of plain paper. The panels can be different sizes or shapes.

2. Find pictures in books or magazines to use for the characters and background.

3. Make copies of the pictures sized to fit in the panels. You might just want to use part of any large photos.

4. Cut out the background images for each panel. Glue the images to the panels.

5. Cut out the characters. Glue them to the panels. Make sure there is room for text next to the characters. If a character extends past the sides of the panel, trim it so it doesn't cover the neighboring panels. Don't worry if a character goes outside the top or bottom of the panel. You will trim it later.

Continued on the next page.

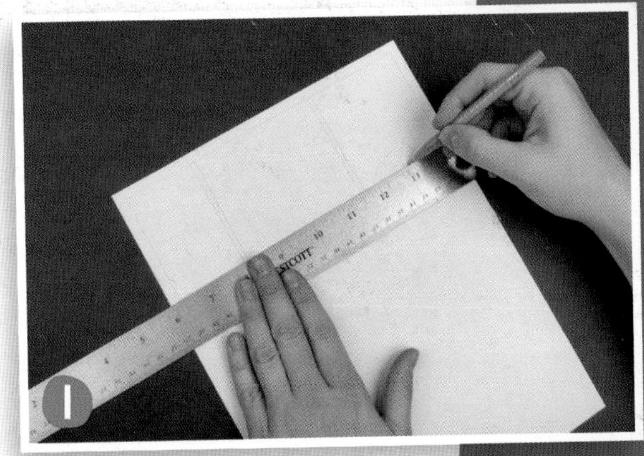
1

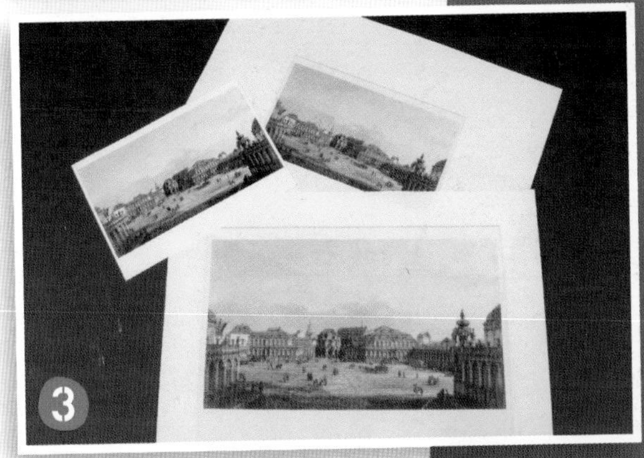
3

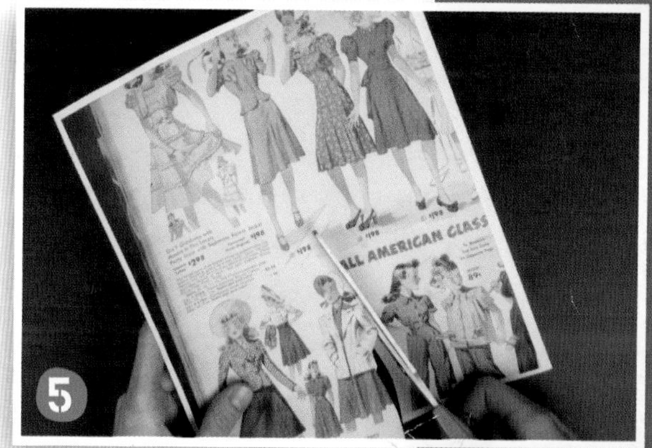
ALL AMERICAN CLASS
5

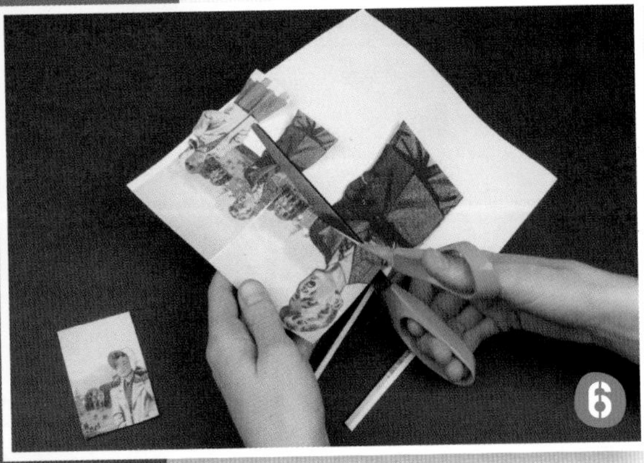

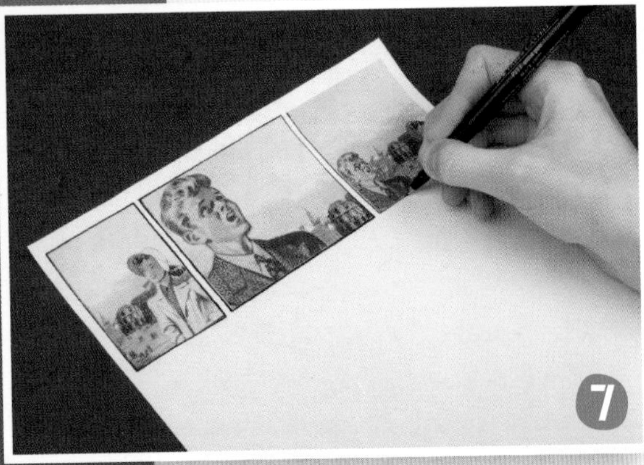

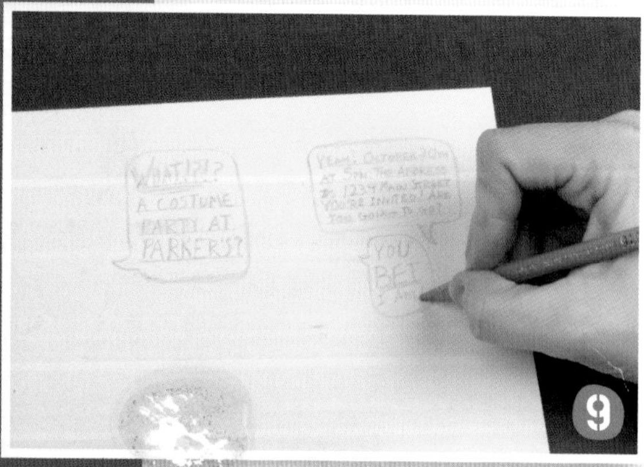
WHAT!?!?
A COSTUME PARTY AT PARKER'S?
YOU BET

6. Cut out each **panel**. Glue the panels near the top of a new sheet of paper.

7. Draw a border around the panel edges with an inking pen.

8. Measure the empty space in each panel. Use the measurements to draw speech bubbles that fit on the panels. Draw them in blue pencil on drawing paper.

9. Write the text for your invitation in the speech bubbles in blue pencil. Have each character say part of the information.

10. Trace over the text and speech bubbles with an inking pen.

11. Cut out each speech bubble. Glue them in place on the **panels**.

12. Make copies of the invitation.

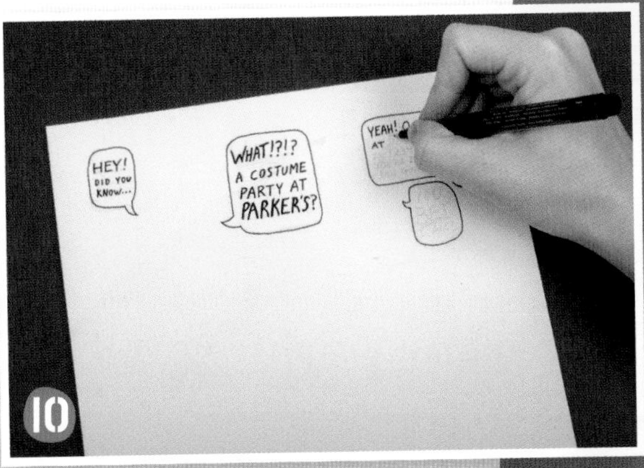
HEY! DID YOU KNOW...
WHAT!?!? A COSTUME PARTY AT PARKER'S?
10

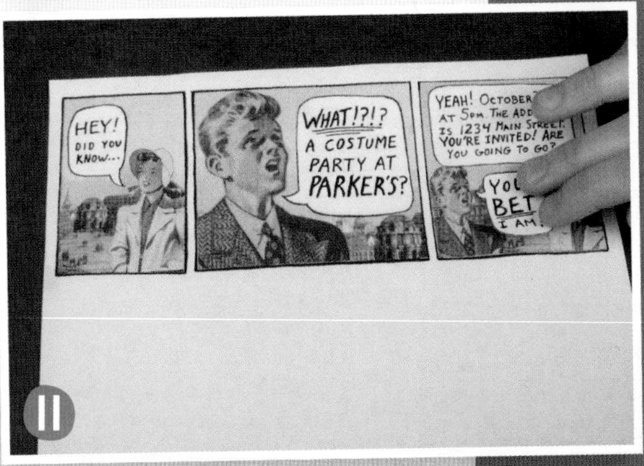
HEY! DID YOU KNOW...
WHAT!?!? A COSTUME PARTY AT PARKER'S?
YOU'RE INVITED! ARE YOU GOING TO GO?
11

TIP Don't waste paper! Try to fit as many invitations as you can on one sheet of paper. After you have made two copies, cut them out and glue them to the original. Use this page to make the rest of the copies.

GRAPHIC NOVEL FOLDER

Make a pocket folder look like an awesome graphic novel!

WHAT YOU NEED

plain paper

pencil

non-glossy paper pocket folder

newspaper

acrylic paint

paintbrushes

black paint pen

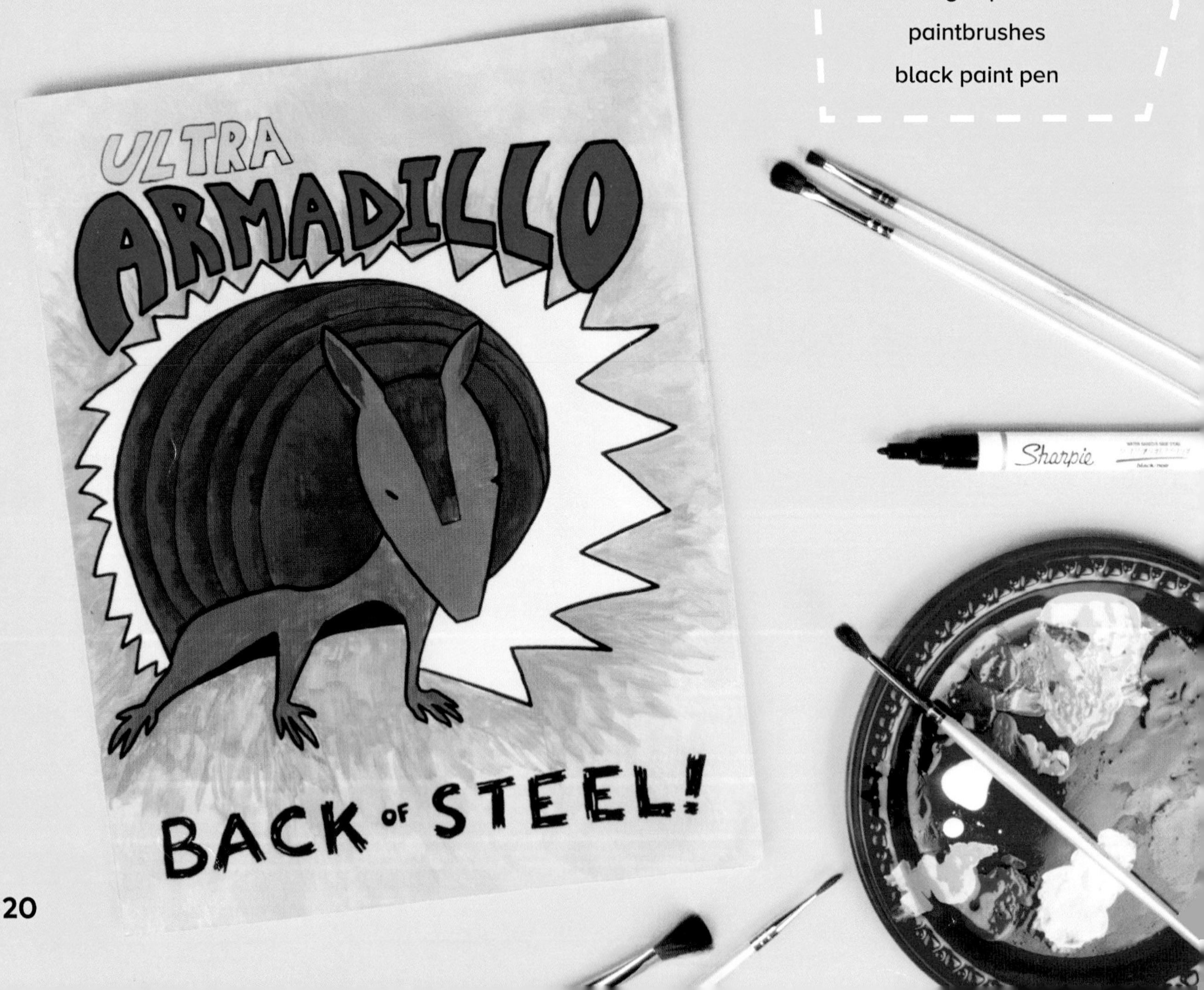
ULTRA
ARMADILLO
BACK OF STEEL!
Sharpie

1. Choose a title and subtitle for your **graphic novel**. Write them on a sheet of plain paper. Write down anything else you want to include on the cover.

2. Draw some rectangular boxes on plain paper. Practice sketching the cover **layout**. Where will the title and subtitle go? What kinds of illustrations do you want to have? Try several different designs.

3. Choose the design you like best. Sketch it on the front of the folder in pencil.

4. Cover your work surface with newspaper. Paint the cover. Start with the background. Then paint the title and illustrations. Let the paint dry.

5. Outline the title and illustrations with black paint pen. Let the paint dry.

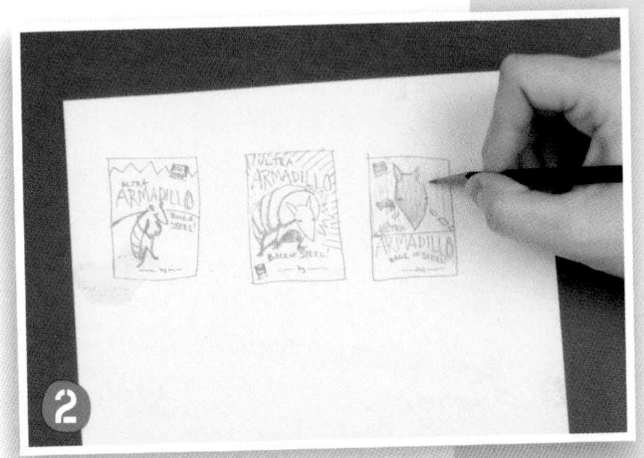
2

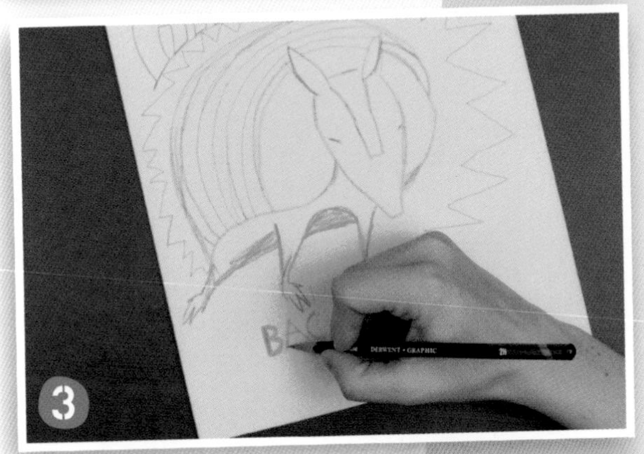
3

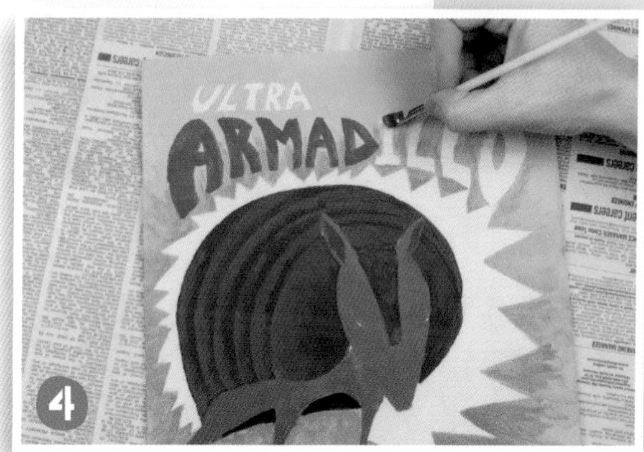
ULTRA
4

STORY PANEL DESIGN

Sharpen your pencils and plan the panels for your own story!

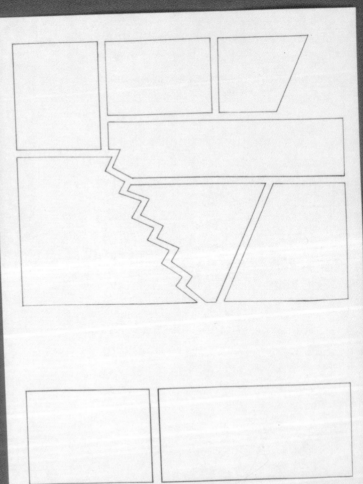

WHAT YOU NEED

pen & notebook or computer, word-processing program & printer

drawing paper

blue pencil · ruler · inking pen

photocopier or scanner & printer

1. Write a story. The story should have 8 to 11 scenes. Add a description of each scene. What will happen? Does the scene use any words, or just show actions? Where does the scene take place? If you're using a computer, print out the story.

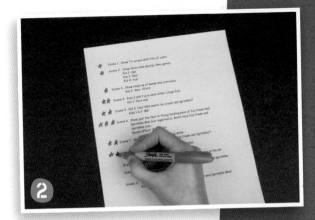

2. Rate the excitement level of each scene using a three-star system. You'll want the most exciting scenes to have **panels** that really stand out.

3. Sketch the panels on drawing paper in blue pencil. Make sure there is a panel for each scene. Use a ruler to draw straight lines. Some of the panels could be angled. Others could be very long or tall. Some might have a jagged edge or no frame at all.

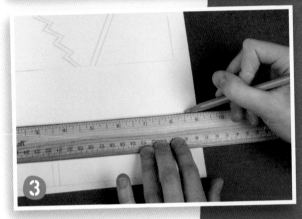

4. Trace over the panel borders with an inking pen.

5. Make several copies of the panel design. Now you're ready to begin sketching speech bubbles and illustrations to tell your story!

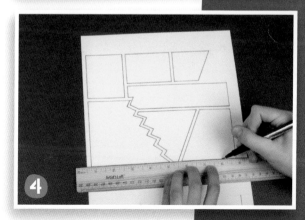

SPLASH! ZING! POW!

Create a comic using only onomatopoeia!

POST
SPLASH
FSSH
FSSH
FSSH
TSCHI TSCHA
TSCHI TSCHA
SPLASH
TSCHI TSCHA
TSCHI TSCHA

WHAT YOU NEED

plain paper

pencil

drawing paper

blue pencil

ruler

inking pen

photocopier or scanner & printer

1. An onomatopoeia is a word that stands for a sound. Examples include "splash," "whoosh," and "ting." Write a story that uses only illustrations and onomatopoeia. Plan how to show the story using scenery, characters and action. Use your imagination and create new words!

2. Practice drawing your onomatopoeia so that each one is different. Can you make the word look the way it sounds? Try writing them in balloons or shapes that help the words look even more like they sound!

3. Use a ruler and blue pencil to create a **panel layout** on drawing paper. See the Story Panel Design project on pages 22 and 23 for ideas.

4. Use the blue pencil to sketch your story and onomatopoeia in the panels.

5. Trace over the pencil lines with an inking pen.

6. Make copies of your comic. Show everyone how much you can say using very few words!

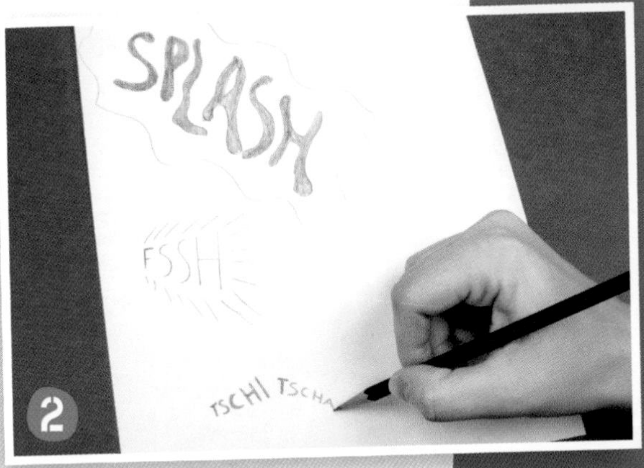
SPLASH
FSSH
TSCHI
2

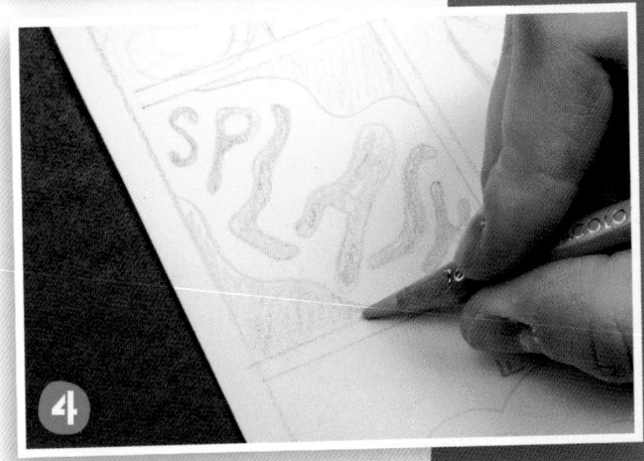
4

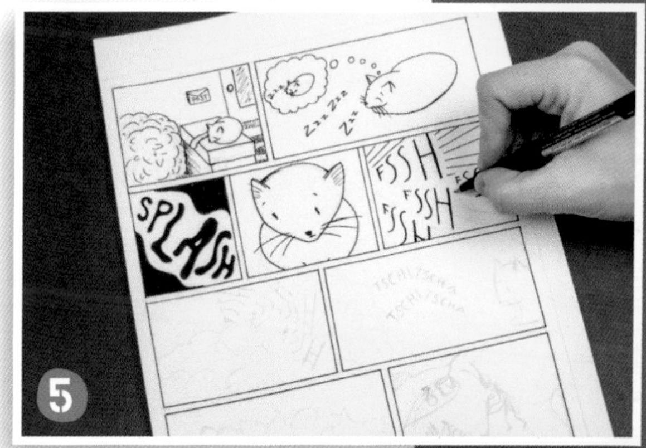
SPLASH
FSSH
FSSH
5

MINI COMIC TIME!

Produce your own eight-page mini comic book to share with your friends!

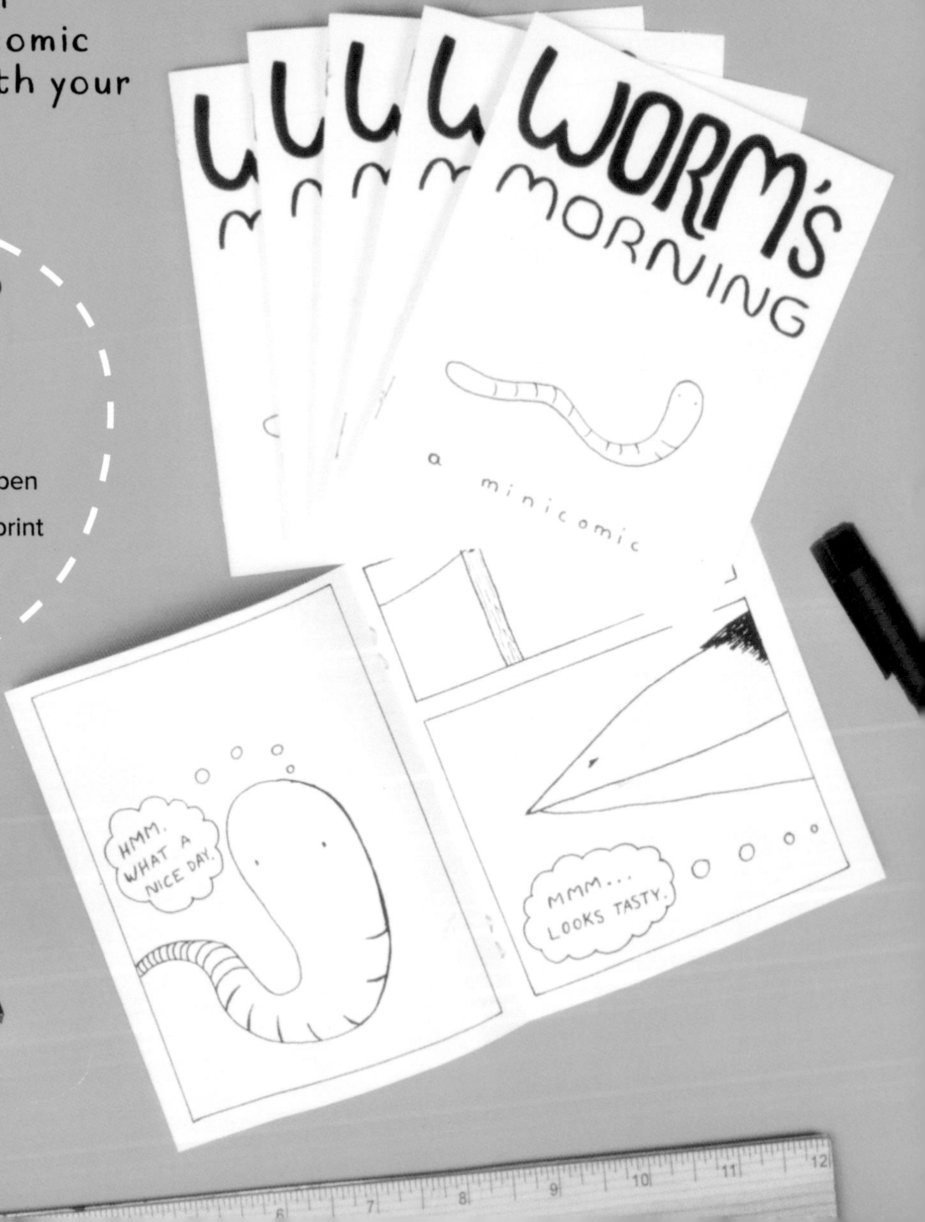
WORM'S MORNING
a minicomic
HMM. WHAT A NICE DAY.
MMM... LOOKS TASTY.

WHAT YOU NEED

drawing paper

scissors • clear tape

notebook • pencil

blue pencil • ruler • inking pen

photocopier that can duplex print (print on both sides)

stapler

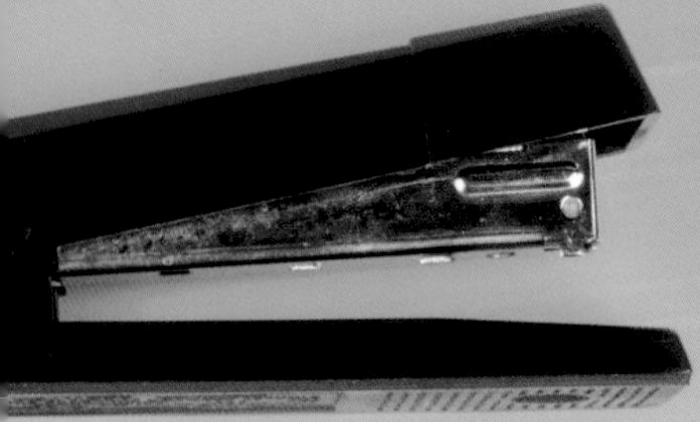

1. Cut a sheet of drawing paper the same size as the paper in your photocopier.

2. Fold the drawing paper in half.

3. Fold the drawing paper in half the other way.

4. Hold the paper by the center fold. Insert the scissors into one short fold and cut the fold. Stop just before you reach the center fold.

5. Unfold the paper. Put a small piece of tape over the top of the center fold. This will keep the pages together.

Continued on the next page.

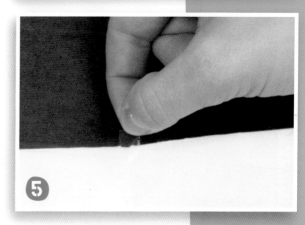

HMM, WHAT A NICE DAY.
MMM... LOOKS TASTY.

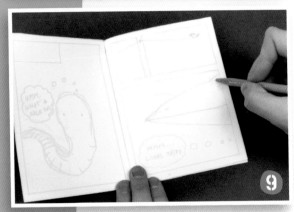

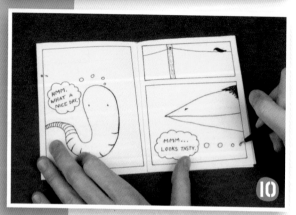

6. Write a story in a notebook. The story should take up six comic-book pages. Some pages might just have one scene. Other pages can be divided into **panels** and have multiple scenes.

7. Write down illustration ideas for the cover and each scene.

8. Sketch the front cover with blue pencil.

9. Sketch the story on the inside pages with blue pencil. Use a ruler to help draw panel borders.

10. Trace over the pencil lines with an inking pen.

11. Unfold the paper. Leave the halves taped together at the top. Use the duplex feature of the photocopier to make copies of your mini comic.

12. Follow steps 2 and 3 to fold each mini comic. Make sure the cover ends up on the front.

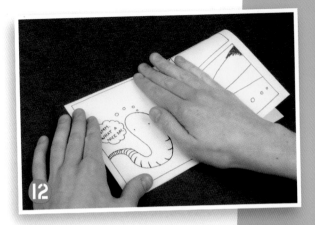

13. Staple each mini comic on its center fold. If the stapler isn't long enough to reach the center fold, gently bend one side of the book.

14. Close the mini comics. Follow step 4 to cut the two top folds of each one.

15. Hand out copies of your mini comic to everyone you know!

HMM. WHAT A NICE DAY!
12

a minicomic
WORM's MORNING
13

TIP Before making many copies of your mini comic, print a test copy. Fold it into a booklet to make sure the copier duplexed it correctly. This can help you avoid wasting a lot of paper.

PLAN A MAKER EVENT!

Being a maker is not just about the finished product. It is about communication, **collaboration**, and creativity. Do you have a project you'd like to make with the support of a group? Then make a plan and set it in action!

SECURE A SPACE

Think of places that would work well for a makerspace. This could be a library, school classroom, or space in a community center. Then, talk to adults in charge of the space. Describe your project. Tell them how you would use the space and keep it organized and clean.

INVITE MAKERS

Once you have a space, it is time to spread the word! Work with adults in charge of the space to determine how to do this. You could make an e-invitation, create flyers about your maker event, or have family and friends tell others.

MATERIALS & TOOLS

Materials and tools cost money. How will you supply these things? **Brainstorm** ways to raise money for your makerspace. You could plan a fund-raiser to buy needed items. You could also ask makers to bring their own supplies.

GLOSSARY

baseline – the imaginary line that letters in a line of type sit on.

brainstorm – to come up with a solution by having all members of a group share ideas.

collaboration – the act of working with another person or group in order to do something or reach a goal.

graphic novel – a story that is presented in comic-strip format and published as a book.

laminate – to cover with a thin layer of clear plastic for protection.

layout – the plan or the design for something, especially printed material such as a newspaper or a book.

panel – a section of a flat surface.

permission – when a person in charge says it's okay to do something.

WEBSITES

To learn more about Cool Makerspace, visit **abdobooklinks.com**. These links are routinely monitored and updated to provide the most current information available.

INDEX